IMAGES
of America

SOUTH BEND
DEFENSE INDUSTRIES

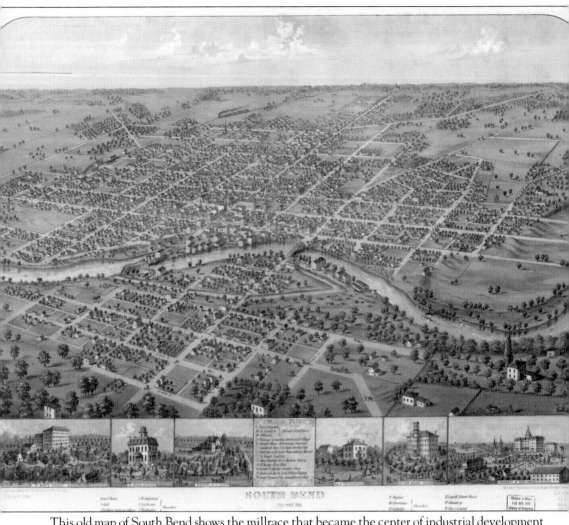

This old map of South Bend shows the millrace that became the center of industrial development in the city and remains a major landmark. (Author's collection.)

ON THE COVER: At the very frontline of America's defense stand our valorous troops and the mighty Humvee, which is built in South Bend, Indiana, by defense contractor AM General Corporation. (Author's collection.)

IMAGES
of America

SOUTH BEND
DEFENSE INDUSTRIES

Patrick R. Foster
Foreword by Congresswoman Jackie Walorski

ARCADIA
PUBLISHING

Published by Arcadia Publishing
Charleston, South Carolina

Printed in the United States of America

Library of Congress Control Number: 2020932851

For all general information, please contact Arcadia Publishing:
Telephone 843-853-2070
Fax 843-853-0044
E-mail sales@arcadiapublishing.com
For customer service and orders:
Toll-Free 1-888-313-2665

Visit us on the Internet at www.arcadiapublishing.com

This book is dedicated to America's warfighters, who protect us from harm.
Your valiant efforts and your sacrifice will never be forgotten.

CONTENTS

ACKNOWLEDGMENTS

I would like to thank Andy Hove, chief executive officer of AM General Corporation, for suggesting this book and for all his considerable help in acquiring materials to make it what it is. More than anyone, he is responsible for the book becoming a reality. I would also like to thank Andy Beckman of the Studebaker National Museum for his substantial help. Travis Childs of the South Bend Historical Society provided a great deal of help with historical information, and I am grateful for that assistance, often supplied on very short notice. All of the images have been added to the Patrick R. Foster Historical Collection, a large, working archive dedicated to the preservation and dissemination of historical information about American Motors, its predecessor companies, and subsidiary and related firms. The Patrick R. Foster Historical Collection is the foremost American Motors archive in the world.

FOREWORD

South Bend and the surrounding area is one of the oldest and most innovative industrial centers in America. South Bend sits atop one of the most important crossroads in America, and the city's founding coincided with the height of first industrial revolution in America and the dawn of the second.

Traces of both the great industrial heritage and ongoing innovation can be seen today at the headwaters of the East Race. The East Race and West Race were built in 1843 to provide power to the textile mills and other industries in South Bend. They later provided hydroelectrical power to industries and the broader community. Today, the community of South Bend and Notre Dame University are building a new, highly advanced, hydroelectrical power system.

The companies in South Bend and the surrounding area have made contributions to almost every industry but none more important than the contributions they have made to the defense industry, our arsenal of democracy, which supports the armed forces of the United States and the armed forces of our allies.

—Jackie Walorski

The modern South Bend headquarters of AM General Corporation reflect its status as a large, important, and longtime supplier to the US military and friendly forces around the globe. AM General is the largest producer of tactical wheeled vehicles in the world.

INTRODUCTION

Although at times it seems that America is a divided nation—north and south, east and west, conservative and progressive, red and blue—the truth is that we are one people working together in the one democracy that has so completely changed the world. As patriotic Americans we understand the importance of American principles such as honesty, loyalty, commitment, dedication, and, above all, honor. We understand that our place in the world is not to act as a dictator or a bully but as a leader with honor that leads by example. America is still the shining beacon of hope for many nations, the one country that others most want to emulate. America exemplifies all that is good in mankind. We welcome the stranger, we help the poor and needy, and we act with malice towards none and with charity for all.

Although America is a peace-loving nation, at times we have had to fight to defend democracy and our very freedom. Many times, we have also gone to war to protect the freedoms of other nations and peoples less fortunate than ourselves. It is especially in times of conflict that Americans forget their differences and come together as one nation, under God, united and indivisible.

Over the many years of our country's existence, a great many American manufacturing companies have had to join the fight as well, working to create and build the armaments of war that are needed to protect our nation. Across the vast expanse of America, the stories are similar—whether in big cities like Detroit and Los Angeles or in hundreds of small company towns, whenever armed conflict has come, the young men of our nation volunteer to take up the battle, while the rest of us stay home and work hard to build them the weapons and equipment they need to win the fight.

One city in particular has come to the country's defense for more years than most people would guess. Lovely South Bend, Indiana, home to Notre Dame University and the Fighting Irish as well as the grand old Studebaker Corporation, AM General Corporation, Bendix, Honeywell, and so many more, has for more than 150 years stepped up whenever it was needed to put the skills and stamina of its people to the ultimate test.

South Bend got its start as a defense industry town during the America Civil War, when the Studebaker brothers were given a subcontract to produce horse-drawn wagons for the Union army. Realizing that the necessary lumber could not be air-dried in time to meet the army's needs, the young men developed an all-new technique for drying the lumber in large kilns. Through such innovation, they were able to build a better, higher-quality wagon at a lower cost and deliver it on time. These wagons and thousands more like them were used to haul food and supplies, transport men home from the battlefield, and serve as ambulances as well. The Studebaker company's corporate descendant is today's AM General Corporation, which builds the mighty Humvee—a vehicle used to transport men and supplies that is also the army's frontline ambulance. Humvees have saved thousands of lives.

Today, South Bend continues to serve as a vital part of the Arsenal of Democracy, standing always to the ready and supplying our warfighters with the equipment needed to keep the world safe.

Here is the South Bend, Indiana, plant of the Bendix Products Division of the mighty Bendix Aviation Corporation in 1940. By this point, the company's employment in South Bend had been expanded to over 5,000 workers producing airplane wheels, brakes, and pneudraulic shock struts; Stromberg auto, aircraft, and marine carburetors; ordnance equipment; and a wide variety of automotive parts.

One

BENDIX CORPORATION AND HONEYWELL AEROSPACE

Vincent Hugo Bendix was the son of Swedish immigrants. A hard-working, born-to-be engineer, in 1907 at the age of 25 he founded the Bendix Corporation in Chicago to manufacture Bendix Motor Buggies. However, the day of the motor buggy was coming to an end, and his firm went bankrupt in 1909. Undaunted, the following year he started a new company to produce an innovative starter drive gear that made the electric starter possible. Later, he invented a new brake system vastly superior to others on the market. In 1929, he founded Bendix Aviation Corporation, and by 1939, its South Bend factory—home of its flagship Bendix Products Division—employed some 3,800 workers producing aircraft brakes, carburetors, and instruments as well as non-aircraft parts and components.

This advertisement from October 1939 says that South Bend–based Bendix Products Division's landing gear equipment provided "Landing Confidence" for combat pilots, clearly illustrating that even then the company was beginning to gear up for defense work. Storm clouds were gathering.

Even before most Americans became aware of the possibility of the country being attacked by the Axis powers, the US military was rapidly preparing for the coming conflict. Employment at Bendix continued to grow by leaps and bounds. The company's 1941 annual report, issued just four days before the murderous attack on Pearl Harbor, stated that Bendix's order backlog stood at $352 million, compared to just $8 million in 1938.

Bendix Aviation bragged of what it called "The Invisible Crew," made up of its dedicated employees and a long list of aircraft products manufactured by various Bendix plants. Gauges, brakes, wheels, magnetos, starter motors, and radios—all were designed and built to aid America's pilots.

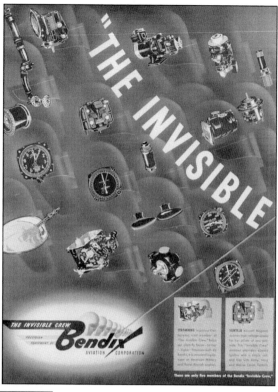

As the advertisement says, by 1942, Bendix Aviation employed more than 40,000 workers in its defense plants, all dedicated to doing their part to win the war. South Bend alone employed some 14,000 during the year, and employment was growing rapidly. During the year, Victor Bendix resigned as president and chief executive officer. To replace him, Ernest Breech, a General Motors vice president and member of the Bendix Board of Directors, was named president.

While nearly every mechanized vehicle the armed forces possessed, including trucks, Jeeps, planes, and ships, were "Bendix equipped," the company's aircraft components were the crown jewel of the firm's operations. Ultra-accurate gauges and instruments, special brakes, high-altitude carburetors, and so much more were supplied by Bendix Aviation.

Bendix Aviation could boast of 15 separate divisions producing instruments and other aircraft equipment. As can be seen in this illustration, Bendix artists deliberately left most of the heavy weaponry out of the picture so that they would not inadvertently provide the enemy with any useful information.

This advertisement from 1943 once again extolls the value of Bendix's Invisible Crew, describing the Bendix Aviation components supplied by the company's various divisions. The Invisible Crew idea was a morale-booster that helped mold Bendix employees into a hard-working, dedicated team. It also instilled more confidence in America's wartime pilots knowing they had so much highly technical equipment at their disposal.

As this advertisement shows, the Invisible Crew was hard at work supporting both air and ground vehicles, including trucks, tanks, and Jeeps, along with virtually every aircraft in the arsenal of the US Army Air Force. In its 1942 annual report, Bendix management stated that its policy was to produce war goods on a limited-profit basis and to refund money to the government whenever cost came down as a result of improved production efficiency. As of September 1942, Bendix had reduced prices on contracts in effect at the beginning of the year by an amazing $123 million and refunded an additional $65 million in profits. One cannot help but wonder if modern corporations would be so generous.

The Bendix Products Division produced a wartime newspaper called the *Bendix Battleline* for employees of its defense plants, as shown here. Within its pages were examples of employees doing their part for the war effort by selling war bonds, suggesting production improvements, or serving in the military. The paper's slogan was "Our battleline is the production line."

During World War II, the giant battleships of the US Navy were the first ever equipped with computers that automatically aimed their big guns with deadly effect. In this unusual advertisement, graphic artists deliberately disguised what the real computer looked like, while copywriters described it as "The Secret Cabinet of 'Captain X'" to make it seem even more mysterious and sensational.

During World War II, Bendix added 700,000 square feet of plant space in South Bend in order to boost production. During fiscal 1942, Bendix Aviation's gross sales tripled to $459 million from $156 million in 1941. Net income actually fell by nearly $1 million, as Bendix patriotically declined to make large profits on war work. The company did begin to set aside funds for reconversion to peacetime and the various costs that would involve.

Planes, tanks, Jeeps, and artillery— Bendix produced parts and components for all of them, making it one of the most important defense contractors in the country. Net sales for 1943 rose to $822 million, a huge increase from the $459 million reported for 1942. Yet even with that large increase in production, the order backlog at the end of the year stood at more than $1 billion! All of Bendix's defense contracts to that time were fixed-price rather than the more lucrative cost-plus type favored by some contractors.

The cultural icon and wartime heroine Rosie the Riveter became a symbol of America's determination to win the war. Thousands of women went to work in defense factories to replace men who had gone off to fight overseas. These tireless American women built the equipment that helped to win the war. Shown here is a woman constructing a wiring system for a vitally needed Bendix Aircraft radio compass.

As a major producer of aircraft brakes, Bendix was called on to supply the needs of America's aircraft manufacturers. Its plants worked around the clock to keep up with demand. From 1941 to 1943, Bendix sales increased 1,448 percent! Sales in 1944 totaled $869 million.

This beautiful Bendix advertisement from 1942 sums up the sense of urgency felt by most Americans early in the war. Great Britain was under attack by the German air force, and the American naval base at Pearl Harbor in Hawaii had been devastated by a Japanese air raid that was launched while the two countries were still at peace. The Allies needed aircraft in numbers previously unheard of, and American workers needed to put in an all-out effort to produce the parts and assemblies to make those planes.

The big pay-off for all the hard work done by thousands of South Bend workers was when the US Army Air Force was able to bring the war to the enemy's shores and inflict extensive damage on its military installations and war production factories.

19

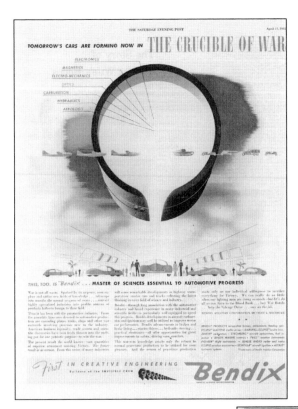

As the war headed towards its inevitable conclusion, Bendix worked to instill hope for the postwar era by noting that the great mechanical advances made while developing war products would carry over to the vehicles of tomorrow. American companies promised a dazzling new future for consumers.

Bendix produced an amazing volume of war goods in the period from 1941 to 1945, including 22 million shell fuses, 22,649 airborne cannons, more than 8 million automotive starter drives, 673,740 Stromberg carburetors, and over $193 million worth of radio equipment. In addition, it produced oxygen regulators, air speed indicators, rate of climb indicators, compasses, and many other aircraft products.

In 1983, Bendix was taken over by Allied Corporation (later known as AlliedSignal), which eventually adopted the Honeywell name. As part of Honeywell International, the company continued to produce components for the military. This photograph shows a Pratt & Whitney J-58 jet engine produced for the SR-71 Blackbird—the fastest plane in the world at the time. Its engine is equipped with a specially developed Bendix fuel control system.

Honeywell is quite diversified. This Bendix CJ-T1 main fuel control was developed for the General Electric F-404 military turbofan engine, used on the F/A-18 A/D aircraft flown by the famed Blue Angels.

America's Air Force and those of many of its allies and friends rely on the avionics and fuel supply components produced by Honeywell and its subsidiaries. Seen here are the YF-23 prototype stealth fighter and B-2 stealth bomber.

This is a closer look at the Bendix CJ-T1 fuel control in the General Electric F-404 turbofan engine used by the Air Force. These powerful engines are installed in the awesome F/A-18 Hornet as well as other planes.

Two

SOUTH BEND LATHE

Producing machine lathes since 1906, South Bend Lathe was a proud company with a fine product that made American manufacturers much more capable and efficient. By 1930, the company had built some 47 percent of the engine-powered lathes in America. When this 1940 advertisement appeared, John J. O'Brien was chairman and Russel E. Frushour was president of the firm. Annual sales were $4.3 million, and a net profit of $634,304 was recorded.

Today You Need SPEED

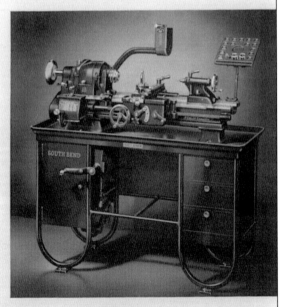

IN YOUR SHOP EQUIPMENT

NOW, more than ever, you need shop machinery that will produce more in less time. High spindle speeds are essential for the efficient use of modern sintered carbide and diamond cutting tools. Smooth, vibration-free operation at high speed is achieved in South Bend Lathes by using a direct belt drive to the spindle, a precision balanced spindle assembly and spindle bearing surfaces that are hardened, ground and superfinished to a smoothness of five micro inches (.000005").

Right—10" Swing, 1" Collet Capacity South Bend Tool Room Precision Bench Lathe. This lathe has nine spindle speeds ranging from 50 to 1357 R. P. M., 1⅜" hole through spindle, 1" maximum collet capacity, 48 power longitudinal carriage feeds, 48 power cross feeds, and cuts 48 different pitches of screw threads.

SIZES OF SOUTH BEND LATHES

Swing	Bed Lengths	Center Distances
9"	3' to 4½'	17" to 35"
10"	3' to 4½'	16⅜" to 34⅜"
13"	4' to 7'	16" to 52"
14½"	5' to 10'	24½" to 84½"
16"	6' to 12'	34" to 106"

PARTIAL LIST OF DEALERS

See a South Bend Lathe before you buy. Write today for free catalog and name of nearest dealer.

Baltimore, Md.—Carey Mach. & Supply
Boston, Mass.—South Bend Lathe Works*
Bridgeport, Conn.—A. C. Bisgood
Buffalo, N.Y.—R. C. Neal Company, Inc.
Chicago, Ill.—South Bend Lathe Works†
Cleveland, Ohio—Reynolds Mach. Co.
Dayton, Ohio—C. H. Gosiger Mach. Co.
Detroit, Mich.—Lee Machinery Company
Los Angeles, Cal.—Eccles & Davies Mach.
Milwaukee, Wis.—W. A. Voell Mach. Co.
Newark, N. J.—J. R. Edwards Mach. Co.

New York, N.Y.—A. C. Colby Mach. Co.
Philadelphia, Pa.—W. B. Rapp, Mach.
Pittsburgh, Pa.—Tracier Mfg. Company
Portland, Ore.—Portland Machinery Co.
Providence, R.I.—Geo. T. Reynolds & Son
Rochester, N. Y.—Ogden R. Adams
St. Paul, Minn.—Robinson, Cary & Sands
San Francisco, Cal.—Moore Mach. Co.
Seattle, Wash.—Star Machinery Company
Syracuse, N.Y.—H. A. Smith, Machinery
York, Pa.—York Machinery & Supply Co.

*Boston Sales Office: 67 Broadway, Kendall Sq., Cambridge, Mass., Tel. Trowbridge 6369
†Chicago Sales Office: Room 308, Machinery Sales Building, Telephone State 7283

SOUTH BEND LATHE WORKS Lathe Builders Since 1906
294 E. Madison Avenue, South Bend, Indiana, U.S.A.

Notice that this October 1940 advertisement features a military plane. Although America was at peace, the Empire of Japan was acting warlike, and the country appeared to be heading into a crisis. Management told stockholders that the company's operations were being affected by the war in Europe as well as unrest in other parts of the world, leading to unprecedented demand for the company's lathes. They were used by the Army and the Navy as well as thousands of customers throughout the country.

One sign of how quickly the situation was developing is seen in this December 1940 advertisement, in which the company displays a shield logo at the lower left stating that it favors adequate preparedness for national defense. The company was in good financial shape with more than $1 million on hand in cash and notes.

This early 1941 advertisement gives a history of lathes as well as an idea of what industries use them. The company introduced its new Series S lathe that same year. When war came, the company would produce essentially the same product, only now all production was going to the war effort. The company's profits for the year rose to $916,890.

25

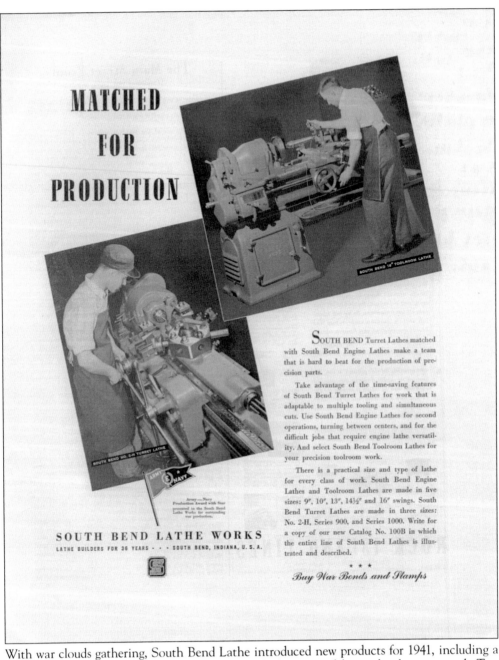

With war clouds gathering, South Bend Lathe introduced new products for 1941, including a new No. 2-H Turret Lathe with power feed created after years of design development work. Two smaller, hand-fed turret lathes were also introduced. The company was awarded the coveted Navy E pennant designation for efficiency and excellence in production.

In this April 1941 advertisement, South Bend Lathe displays its most popular lathes. The nation was still at peace, but it was a tenuous, stressful period in American history.

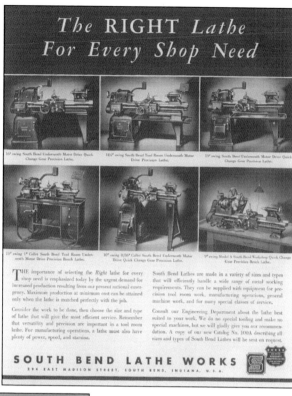

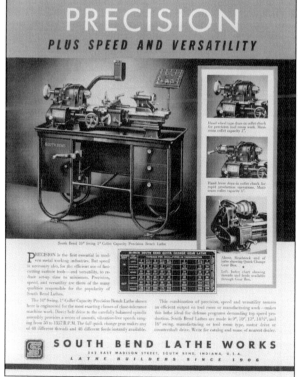

Despite ongoing tensions throughout the world, this August 1941 advertisement gives no indication that the nation was busy rearming itself as a precaution even as it tried to negotiate with an increasingly militaristic Japan. South Bend Lathe employed about 900 workers at the time.

Once the Empire of Japan attacked the United States deliberately and without warning, the country was plunged into war. South Bend Lathe's advertising efforts then began to extol the idea that America's defense workers were a crucial part of the war effort, as seen in this sample advertisement.

The Man at the Lathe Fights Too!

... and every turn of the spindle, as he guides his work through many precision operations, helps bring Victory one step closer.

Hours spent at a lathe may lack the dangerous excitement of combat—but the valorous men on the battle fronts breathe a prayer of thankfulness for guns, shells, planes, tanks—for all the superb equipment which is helping them swing the tide against the Axis.

So the man at the lathe is a soldier, too, as he braces his shoulders to the task of pouring out weapons in an ever-increasing stream. He faces his task grimly...proudly...proclaiming by the gleam in his eye and the jut of his jaw that he will not be outdone in service to his country, and knowing that America's production is a decisive factor in the war.

To help America "tool up for Victory" the output of South Bend Lathes has been increased (we can't say how much) in the last year and a half—giving the man at the lathe the efficient, dependable production weapon he must have to win.

There is a South Bend Lathe for every class of work—engine lathes, toolroom lathes, and turret lathes. Write now for our new catalog No. 100H in which the entire line of lathes is illustrated and described.

SOUTH BEND LATHE WORKS
LATHE BUILDERS FOR 36 YEARS
SOUTH BEND, INDIANA

South Bend Lathe's profits fell somewhat during the 1942 fiscal year, as the company invested $340,000 in the construction of a large addition to its plant in order to keep up with the orders flooding in. Many employees were volunteering to serve in the armed forces.

KEEPING *Precision* IN PACE WITH PRODUCTION

WAR production demands precision from start to finish—from toolroom to production shop. Without precision, the vast quantities of war supplies so urgently needed could not be produced in time—for efficient mass production is based on a degree of precision which permits the perfect interchangeability of thousands of duplicate units.

Because of their dependable precision, South Bend Lathes have long been favorites in the toolroom. For this same reason, plus a fatigueless ease of operation, they have been equally popular for manufacturing operations. And now South Bend Turret Lathes are stepping up production in the shops of hundreds of war industries—with no sacrifice in precision.

South Bend Toolroom Lathes and Engine Lathes are made in five sizes: 9", 10", 13", 14½" and 16" swing. South Bend Turret Lathes are made in three sizes: 900 Series, 1000 Series, and No. 2-H. Write for catalog and name of nearest dealer.

SOUTH BEND LATHE WORKS
LATHE BUILDERS FOR 36 YEARS   SOUTH BEND, INDIANA, U.S.A.

South Bend Lathe's new addition consisted of a four-story-and-basement structure of just under 60,000 square feet. The new building, attached to the existing plant, was granted accelerated depreciation and would be amortized in five years or less. This was allowed due to the wartime necessity of building up production volume.

Once America got into action, its vast tank armies were in need of periodic service and repair. Mobile machine shops, staffed by gallant and skilled technicians, often stayed close to the front lines in order to effect needed repairs. South Bend Lathes provided one of its most important machines. During 1943, nearly 300 South Bend Lathe employees were serving in the military.

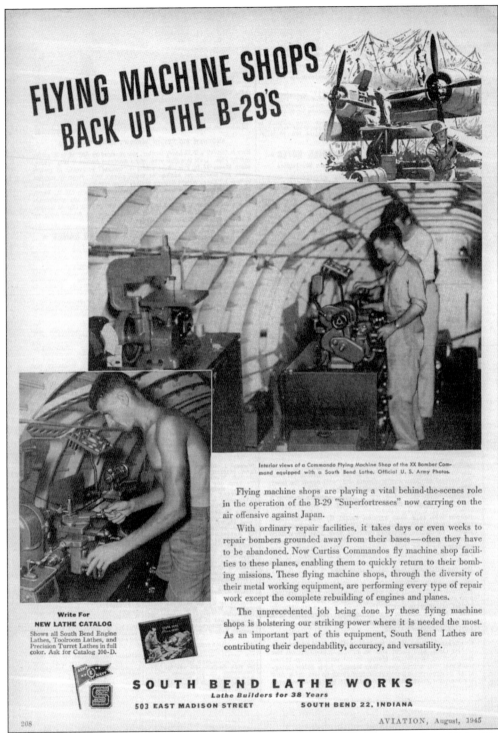

FLYING MACHINE SHOPS BACK UP THE B-29'S

Interior views of a Commando Flying Machine Shop of the XX Bomber Command equipped with a South Bend Lathe. Official U. S. Army Photos.

Flying machine shops are playing a vital behind-the-scenes role in the operation of the B-29 "Superfortresses" now carrying on the air offensive against Japan.

With ordinary repair facilities, it takes days or even weeks to repair bombers grounded away from their bases—often they have to be abandoned. Now Curtiss Commandos fly machine shop facilities to these planes, enabling them to quickly return to their bombing missions. These flying machine shops, through the diversity of their metal working equipment, are performing every type of repair work except the complete rebuilding of engines and planes.

The unprecedented job being done by these flying machine shops is bolstering our striking power where it is needed the most. As an important part of this equipment, South Bend Lathes are contributing their dependability, accuracy, and versatility.

Write For
NEW LATHE CATALOG
Shows all South Bend Engine Lathes, Toolroom Lathes, and Precision Turret Lathes in full color. Ask for Catalog 100-D.

SOUTH BEND LATHE WORKS
Lathe Builders for 38 Years
503 EAST MADISON STREET   SOUTH BEND 22, INDIANA

South Bend Lathes were even put to use in the so-called "flying machine shops" established in Curtiss Commando airplanes, which flew skilled machinists and their lathes to repair broken aircraft wherever needed, greatly speeding up their return to combat.

Three

STUDEBAKER CORPORATION

Studebaker was one of the oldest transportation companies in America, having built its first covered wagon in 1852. With the onset of the American Civil War, Studebaker became an important defense manufacturer producing various wagons for the Union army.

The bearded Studebaker brothers made their fortunes building wagons and buggies for farmers, businessmen, and the military. The company became the largest maker of horse-drawn wagons in the world and an important defense contractor during the Civil War, Boer War, Spanish-American War, World Wars I and II, the Korean War, and the Vietnam War. The record is probably unequaled by any other American firm.

Here, a long line of Union wagons enters the town of Petersburg, Virginia, during 1865, toward the end of the Civil War. The Union army under General Grant had been trying to capture Richmond and Petersburg since 1864.

This photograph, from the archives of the Studebaker National Museum, is labeled "Studebaker gun carriages for the China War" but is undated. It may refer to the Boxer Rebellion of 1899–1901, in which American troops were part of an eight-nation coalition sent to defend foreigners who were being attacked by militants.

In World War I, horse-drawn wagons were still the primary movers of military equipment—motor trucks were just coming into popular use. Here, a Studebaker-built military wagon produced for the US Army has been put into service to support Field Battery B. Note the heavy-duty construction.

During World War I, the Studebaker Corporation was an important supplier of gun carriages to the US Army. This photograph shows the part of the Studebaker plant where the shield and spade assemblies were installed on the carriages. It is interesting how clean and well-lit this assembly room is.

Another view of gun carriage assembly, this photograph shows Studebaker's Cradle Assembly Department, where the guns were mounted onto the cradles. Note the date: September 26, 1918.

Dated September 19, 1918, this photograph shows the fixture used for milling the traversing transom for a carriage meant to mount a 4.7-inch gun. This particular carriage is a Studebaker Model 1906.

Once the gun carriage was completely assembled and painted, it was ready for shipping. This is the Model 1906 4.7-inch gun carriage, used in World War I.

This is the business end of a Studebaker gun carriage complete with gun and a shield to protect the gunners. Note the camouflage paint.

Here is a fully assembled Studebaker gun carriage as it is displayed at a war bond rally in downtown South Bend. Note the large sign on the right of the photograph. Although it is partly cut off, it is a note of encouragement to General Pershing, the commander of the American Expeditionary Force, the first US troops to land in France.

In addition to gun carriages and artillery wagons, Studebaker also produced mine anchors for the Allies during World War I. Here is a side view of one of the mine anchors.

The mine anchors produced by Studebaker were used to keep mines at just the right depth to do the most damage to enemy vessels and were mainly a defensive weapon to protect harbors and keep enemy ships out of Allied shipping lanes.

A great many young men lost their lives during World War I, and many more were wounded. To carry medical aid to these unfortunate men and to help evacuate them when needed, the US Army ordered thousands of horse-drawn ambulances from Studebaker. Here is a group of such ambulances ready for shipment.

Pictured are Studebaker ambulances produced for the Spanish-American War. This period photograph shows a long line of ambulances being shipped by rail. Note that the canvas tops have been installed. Note too the Studebaker Brothers sign on the building in the background.

During World War I, the Army purchased a great many of these sprinkler wagons from Studebaker. The function of the wagons was to sprinkle water on the road surface to help keep down dust. When thousands of men are on the march, the dust clouds they kick up can be a terrific impediment to efficient moving, not to mention they choked both men and horses.

Produced for the Army Quartermaster Corps, the sprinkler wagons rode ahead of the troops to wet the roadbed. These wagons carried a very heavy load and were built to be extra sturdy.

A contingent of sprinkler wagons ready for shipment gives an idea of the large orders placed for these vehicles. Sprinkler wagons were also purchased by municipalities to help keep down dust in cities and towns. This, of course, was in the days before macadam came into common use in America.

A trainload of 24 Studebaker sprinkler wagons, most likely heading for France or the killing fields of Flanders on the western front, awaits shipment at a siding in South Bend.

One of the worst parts of war in France was the muddy roads that bogged down transportation. To combat this, Studebaker designed and built this tractor, which was used to haul big guns. The horse-drawn wagons and caissons normally used for this work often got stuck in the endless mud.

This is another view of a Studebaker military ambulance for World War I. One wonders how many of these have survived out of the thousands that were produced.

During World War I, South Bend held a war bond rally to encourage people to purchase bonds to help finance the war effort. Here, a horse-drawn cart is set up with a large cannon shell, probably made of cardboard or papier mâché, with a sign reading "A Pill for Kaiser Bill," a reference to German leader Kaiser Wilhelm.

Another horse-drawn Studebaker wagon featured in that same parade in South Bend was this camouflaged military ambulance complete with a nurse.

This parade float commemorates the SS *Tuscania*, a troopship carrying American servicemen to France during the Great War. On board were over 2,000 American servicemen and a crew of 384. A German submarine sank it and, although nearby ships were able to save most of the men, some 121 American servicemen were killed. Other estimates claim as many as 200 men drowned.

Where are the horses to pull this thing? In all likelihood, this particular display was mounted on a motorized Studebaker chassis. In any event, the message is clear.

During the period just before World War II broke out in Europe, the Empire of Japan was acting aggressively in the Pacific, and countries like Australia began to prepare for the possibility of war. The Nanking Massacre of 1937 demonstrated clearly how brutal and vicious the Japanese army was. This 1938 Studebaker ambulance was in the service of the Royal Australian Navy.

Before America was drawn into World War II, the country helped its future allies with a program in which it loaned trucks, tanks, ships, and weapons at no cost. Known as Lend-Lease, it saved Britain and Russia when they had their backs to the wall. In this photograph, Russian women admire a Studebaker truck provided under the Lend-Lease Act.

Studebaker was contracted by the US War Department to produce heavy-duty military trucks for the US Army and its allies. Here is one of the many thousands of these trucks that were produced on the assembly line in South Bend.

This 1942 Studebaker army truck is fitted with a troop carrier body and could also be used for hauling supplies to the front. Note the excellent ground clearance and rugged construction. These trucks were built to conquer the worse terrain imaginable.

No war front is too tough for these powerful heavy-duty Studebakers

A wartime Studebaker advertisement from 1942 shows a fleet of tough Studebaker trucks undergoing cold-weather maneuvers. The trucks were built to overcome such weather, and thousands of them were shipped to the Russian army under America's Lend-Lease program. Note the "Buy U.S. War Bonds" message at the bottom of the page.

Studebaker trucks "take to the air" in the service of the Red Army

As this wartime advertisement states, a substantial portion of the six-by-six and six-by-four 2.5-ton Studebaker trucks sent to Russia during the war were Studebakers. The Russians appreciated the Studebakers' extraordinary stamina in the fierce Russian climate.

Beginning in January 1941, Studebaker was given contracts by the US War Department and Defense Plant Corporation to construct and equip three plants in which to build military aircraft engines. In the years following, Studebaker built well over 60,000 of the complex Cyclone aircraft engines used in the Boeing Flying Fortress.

One of the more unusual military products designed and built by Studebaker engineers was this imitation army tank. Created in 1942, when a shortage of real tanks existed, the fake tank was used to train tank crews for the vehicles they would eventually be using.

Although best-known for its army trucks, Studebaker made a vital contribution to the war effort when it designed, engineered, and built the famed tracked vehicle shown here. Officially known as the M-29 Cargo Carrier, it was soon nicknamed the "Weasel."

After receiving the assignment to design and produce a tracked cargo carrier, Studebaker engineers built the first Weasel in just 34 days. Designed to haul men and equipment over any kind of terrain, it could cross streams with ease. Powered by a Studebaker Champion engine, it was used extensively in the Pacific islands campaign.

Like the Army Jeep, it seemed that nothing could stop a Studebaker Weasel. Many of these vehicles have been saved and restored by collectors. They are often seen at meetings of the Studebaker Drivers Club.

I've been driving a "Champion"... that's why I'm going to buy one

IT'S a seasoned young ski trooper from New England, later an infantryman, who is doing the talking.

"Why a Champ?" he asks. "I've been driving its twin brother, that's why. A Studebaker Weasel. That little job sure proved to be a ski trooper's best pal for two tough winters in the mountains during the war. That baby can go anywhere. And they tell me, that in a car, its Champion engine saves a guy a lot of money on gas."

Yes, many men still in the services as well as milli of other Americans have their hearts set on those smart new Skyway Style Champions that Studebaker is now building.

Thanks to Studebaker engineering genius, Studebaker's unusual competence in production and Studebaker's unique father-and-son craftsmanship, this new and finer Studebaker Champion paces all other leading lowest price cars in all around savings per mile.

Studebaker
South Bend 27, Indiana, U. S. A.

PIONEER AND PACEMAKER IN AUTOMOTIVE PROGRESS

The Weasel was a "Champion" in action—designed by Studebaker engineers—built in the Studebaker factories

© 1945 The Studebaker Corporation

In addition to the Pacific theater of war, the sturdy Weasels were used in the winter snowfields of Europe, as attested to in this advertisement that highlights the connections between the prewar Studebaker Champion automobile and the Weasel, which used a Champion engine for motive power along with the Champion's clutch and transmission.

Another Studebaker advertisement, this one from 1944, shows the mighty Weasels clawing their way through the jungle on some Pacific island carrying troops and vital supplies. The amphibious Weasels were initially tested in the St. Joseph River in South Bend.

Studebaker trucks were used around the world during World War II, from the steaming jungles of the Pacific to the hot desert sands of Arabia and the frozen fields of Russia. As Studebaker claimed: "The roadways of the world are worn deep by Studebaker wheel marks."

Seen here in 1942 is a Studebaker army truck built for hauling cargo or troops. With six-by-six drive, these tough trucks could climb just about any hill they were likely to come across.

The proudest assignment in our 90-year history

Studebaker builds wright cyclone engines for the Flying Fortress

★ STUDEBAKER'S 90TH ANNIVERSARY 1852-1942 ★

As this Studebaker advertisement proclaims, building the mighty Wright Cyclone aircraft engines for the awesome Boeing Flying Fortress bombers was "The proudest assignment in our 90-year history." Studebaker had been founded in 1852 by the Studebaker brothers, blacksmiths in South Bend.

More and more Flying Fortresses are powered by Studebaker-built Cyclone engines

Clear-eyed, clean-hearted young Americans are up there in those Flying Fortresses—writing new chapters of a free world's destiny. Many of them were carefree school boys only yesterday. Today, they're pouring cringing fear into the souls of once boastful "supermen." To these gallant youngsters—and to their expert crews below that keep them flying—we of Studebaker pledge ourselves to go on producing more and still more of the mighty Wright Cyclone engines for these devastating Boeing bombers. We'll "give more than we promise" in the best Studebaker tradition. Meanwhile, civilian needs must and will wait . . . until Studebaker completes this wartime assignment . . . until the finer Studebaker motor cars and motor trucks of the brighter days of Victory can be built.

BUY U.S. WAR BONDS

Big Studebaker military trucks stand out in all the major war zones—Besides producing many Flying Fortress engines, Studebaker is also one of the largest builders of multiple-drive military trucks. We're proud of our assignments in arming our Nation and its Allies.

Awarded to Aviation Division of The Studebaker Corporation

Studebaker BUILDS WRIGHT CYCLONE ENGINES FOR THE BOEING *Flying Fortress*

Although Studebaker was not the sole source for the vitally important Wright Cyclone engines, it was one of the major suppliers. Each engine required more than 8,000 parts, 80,000 separate machining operations, and 50,000 different inspections. Note the small mention of the Army's E award, given to Studebaker's Aviation Division for outstanding aircraft engine production.

"Betcha Dad worked on those engines!"

They're talking about a Flying Fortress powered by Studebaker-built Wright Cyclone engines

JUST a little while back, expert machinist John H. Williams and his two sons, Evard and John, were working together at Studebaker.

Today they're still working together in spirit—but many miles apart.

The father is building Wright Cyclone engines for the mighty Boeing Flying Fortress in the Studebaker factory. The boys have hung up their working clothes to put on the fighting uniforms of Uncle Sam.

Two on the firing line—one on the production line—each still giving "more than he promised"—each doing everything he can do to make victory sure.

There are many families such as the Williams family whose names shine brightly these war days on the Studebaker roster—

families that are steadfastly maintaining the great Studebaker father-and-son tradition at home or far away.

And when the fighting job is done, that tradition will be carried forward, you may be sure, in finer Studebaker motor cars and motor trucks than ever for civilian use. The solid principles upon which Studebaker craftsmanship has been founded will remain unchanged.

STUDEBAKER

Builder of Wright Cyclone engines
for the Boeing Flying Fortress, big multiple-
drive military trucks and other
vital war matériel

Craftsman father of craftsmen sons

John H. Williams, father of soldiers Evard and John, has been with Studebaker 21 years. He is one of many Studebaker veterans whose aptitude for fine work influenced and inspired their sons to become Studebaker craftsmen, too. Every Studebaker employee is proud of his organization's assignments in the arming of our Nation and its Allies.

As this advertisement shows, Studebaker employees, both those involved in defense manufacturing and those younger men serving in the military, were rightly proud of the fine contribution Studebaker craftsmen made to America's war program.

Studebaker advertisements sometimes mentioned specific employees by name, as in this one from 1944. Milan Balaban worked in the Studebaker plant prior to enlisting in the US Navy, where he was assigned to a Construction Battalion (abbreviated CB and known as the Seabees). His father, Joe, who still worked at the plant, had another son and daughter serving in the Navy.

The brute strength and stamina of the Studebaker army trucks was wonderful to behold, and they made a reputation for themselves. They were so sturdy, in fact, that the Russian army continued to use them for decades after the war ended. Studebaker produced 197,678 military trucks during World War II.

After World War II ended, Studebaker resumed production of civilian cars and trucks and went on to great success in both fields. However, by June 1950, the US Army was preparing for war on the Korean Peninsula, so Studebaker was given a contract for production of military trucks. The design settled on was this, dubbed the M-108, seen equipped for wrecker duty.

Like the truck shown above, this Studebaker-built gasoline truck was produced in 1952. It is an M-49 model. The canvas roof was specified to make it easier to ship. The company also prepared to undertake production of jet engines for the US Air Force.

This 1952 M-109 army truck, produced by Studebaker, is equipped with a special body for use as an officer's (usually a general's) mobile headquarters. Note the opening side windows and ladder for access to rooftop storage.

Here is a rear view of the 1952 M-109 Mobile Command Center truck seen above. Entrance is via the steps leading to the dual rear doors. The six-by-six chassis ensures that the general and his staff can be taken right up to the front lines if necessary.

During 1961, Studebaker received a new order for 5,000 two-and-a-half-ton military trucks. It had received orders for 5,037 trucks in 1957 and another 5,031 in 1958, so this had become a profitable, continuing business. Seen here is one of the Studebaker-produced army trucks, this one equipped for hauling men and supplies. Note the different road wheels compared to the earlier models.

Another c. 1961 Studebaker army truck, this one has been produced with a heavy-duty rack body for hauling men and equipment. Seeking to grow the company into other markets, Studebaker established its Defense Products Division this year to focus more attention on military business.

This interesting press photograph shows a load of Studebaker army trucks, including two tractors and two straight jobs. Note the new Studebaker cars and trucks in this marshalling yard.

A different view of the same trainload of army trucks shows a load of new Mercedes-Benz cars also being readied for shipment. At the time, Studebaker was the distributor of Mercedes-Benz cars in the United States and Canada as well for DKW and Auto Union cars.

Here is a 1962 military truck on the assembly line at Studebaker. Note that this particular unit is being produced for the US Air Force. Notice how modern, clean, and well-lighted this factory looks; it was Studebaker's newest plant at the time.

By 1962, Studebaker's defense production was mainly undertaken in its Chippewa Avenue plant in South Bend. Consisting of approximately 1.56 million square feet of floor area, it was a modern, single-story plant of steel and masonry construction with a 12-inch double-reinforced floor—and it was completely air-conditioned as well.

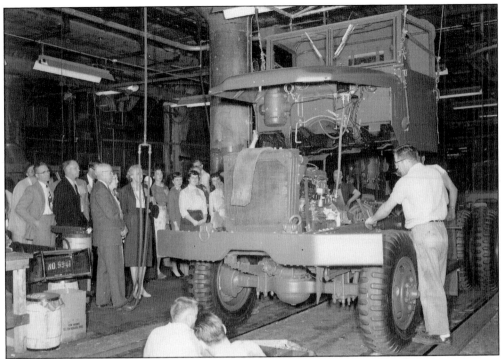

This appears to be some sort of special event—perhaps the startup on a new truck contract or new model. The vehicle's cab is being gently lowered onto the completed chassis.

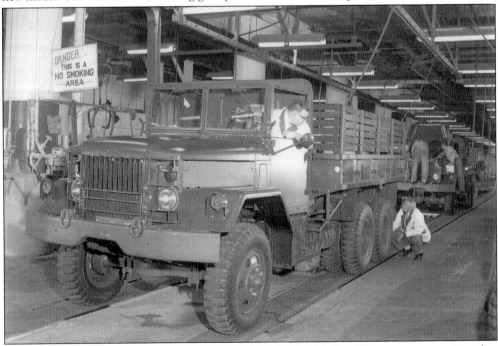

Here is the final inspection line for army trucks built by Studebaker. The company continued to receive new contracts for army trucks and continued to build them, but the clock was running out on Studebaker's automotive business.

These are military tractor trucks coming down the line in South Bend, probably among the last to be produced by Studebaker. In December 1963, the company made a sad announcement: automobile production in South Bend was coming to an end. From 1964 on, all Studebaker cars would be built in Canada. The decision was made to also exit the military truck business at about the same time.

This photograph was taken in a marshalling yard towards the very end of Studebaker's time as a supplier of military trucks. The trucks are parked in neat rows; about half of them are painted olive drab green, the rest are painted a bright red. It is difficult to understand why Studebaker would give up the military business: the contract it had on hand called for production of 8,634 big five-ton trucks, valued at $81 million. The passenger cars seen here are 1964 model-year Studebakers, produced before the main plant shut down on December 21, 1963.

Four

KAISER JEEP CORPORATION

In 1964, Studebaker sold its South Bend military truck plant to Kaiser Jeep Corporation, and the Army agreed to a novation agreement assigning Studebaker's existing truck contracts to the Kaiser organization. This photograph shows the signing of that agreement. From left to right are (first row) Homer Kelly of Kaiser; Maj. Gen. A.K. Sibley; James Currie of Kaiser; and Col. Frank Havel, project manager, General Purpose Vehicle; (second row) Paul Zalecki of Kaiser; Col. Mario Maffeo, Judge Advocate Office; Ralph Schneider of Kaiser; Charles Pagano, contracting officer, Chicago Procurement District; and L. Kent, legal advisor, MOCOM Judge Advocate Office.

During 1964, Kaiser Jeep Corporation's government sales rose for the third year in a row, to $78.145 million, which was more than double the figure of just two years previous. The lion's share of this increase was a result of acquiring Studebaker's military truck business. Seen here is one of the final trucks produced by Studebaker, virtually identical to the trucks that were to be produced by Kaiser Jeep in the same Chippewa Avenue plant.

NOW *from the producer*
of **Jeep** *vehicles...*

HEAVY DUTY
6×6 TRUCKS

KAISER Jeep CORPORATION
TOLEDO, OHIO 43601

Kaiser Jeep dubbed its new military truck operation the South Bend Division. As a result of competitive bidding undertaken since the Kaiser takeover, the South Bend Division had been awarded orders for additional five-ton trucks, along with two-and-a-half-ton trucks. By mid-1964, the company had a backlog of orders for more than 40,000 vehicles, which would call for production through September 1967.

When it acquired the South Bend Plant and signed the novation agreement, Kaiser Jeep's new division had a backlog of orders for two-and-a-half-ton trucks. Although Kaiser Jeep's home plant in Toledo, Ohio, was huge, the South Bend plant had been designed for efficient military production and was better suited by far. It was not long before Kaiser Jeep was able to win an additional contract for the production of heavy-duty five-ton military trucks, including the wrecker seen here.

Another important model in the M39 series of five-ton trucks was this M51 heavy-duty dump truck. From 1964 to 1969, Kaiser Jeep built nearly 45,000 of the M39 series trucks.

This tough-looking prime mover is the M52A2 five-ton truck, built for hauling heavy loads over long distances. This truck was built around 1965. With the Vietnam War growing in intensity, the Army needed more tactical trucks of every description. By the end of the year, the backlog of government orders was a whopping $330 million.

Here is the final assembly line for five-ton trucks in South Bend. These trucks featured folding canvas tops, folding windshields, and frameless door glass so that they could be shipped with their tops down, which helped them to fit into ship holds as well as certain aircraft.

Pictured is the M55 five-ton hauler. To illustrate the rapid increase in government orders for military trucks, sales by Kaiser Jeep Corporation to military and civilian agencies of the US government during fiscal 1968 totaled more than $297 million. While a portion of this was for civilian vehicles, the bulk of the business was military production.

The South Bend plant had its own test track and proving grounds so that vehicles could be road tested before shipment. This is a Kaiser Jeep five-ton cargo truck on the test track at Chippewa Avenue.

With the addition of the South Bend Division, Kaiser Jeep became the largest producer of tactical wheeled vehicles to the US Army and probably the largest military truck producer in the world. The former Studebaker plant was relatively new and efficiently laid out for specialty vehicle production.

Sales of government-destined trucks continued to climb during 1967, as the renamed Defense and Government Products Division received a new Army contract for additional two-and-a-half-ton trucks.

During 1968, the Vietnam War was raging, and the demand for military trucks was at its highest point since the Korean War. As always, South Bend stepped up to the task and produced the needed vehicles.

Kaiser Jeep's South Bend factory also produced large numbers of vehicles for the US Postal Service, including this FJ-6 half-ton unit. Like other postal trucks, these were considered dual-purpose; in case of attack or natural disasters, they were to be pressed into service as civil defense vehicles.

Kaiser Jeep trucks were not used just for warfare. As this photograph taken in Birmingham, Alabama, illustrates, the Army often sent its heavy-duty trucks to help in local civilian emergencies.

Dated October 20, 1969, this photograph shows the signing of a new contract for 26,701 two-and-a-half-ton military trucks to be built in South Bend. Pictured from left to right are (seated) Maj. Frank Szustak; (standing) Ralph W. Schneider, a longtime Kaiser Jeep executive; Col. C.E. Kinkel; and John Razinski.

Five

AM GENERAL CORPORATION

This aerial view shows the Kaiser Jeep South Bend military vehicle factory as it looked in late 1969, when the company was being taken over by American Motors. This is the same plant Studebaker owned; the products it built had been passed on to Kaiser Jeep and then AM General, a division of American Motors. The line of succession from Studebaker's military production to AM General's is quite clear and essentially linear. Today, AM General and its predecessor companies can boast more than 150 years of service to the nation.

The M151 Mutt tactical truck was created to replace the wartime Jeep. Ford Motor Company designed the original Mutt, but by the late 1960s, Kaiser Jeep's South Bend Division had won the contract to produce them. AM General continued to build them for years. Shown here around 1972 is an updated version, known as the M151A2, which featured improvements to the suspension.

The improved M151A2 can easily be identified by the front turn lamps, which are set in drop-down pockets in the fenders. The series also included the M825 106-millimeter rifle carrier. From 1972 to 1985, AM General produced more than 81,000 of these vehicles in the South Bend plant.

Shown here on the cover of *Automotive Industries* magazine is Cruse W. Moss, the first head of AM General and reportedly the man who named the company. Moss is shown with a range of AM General products, though not the entire product range by far. Previous to AM General, Moss had been an executive with Kaiser Jeep Corporation's Special Products Division.

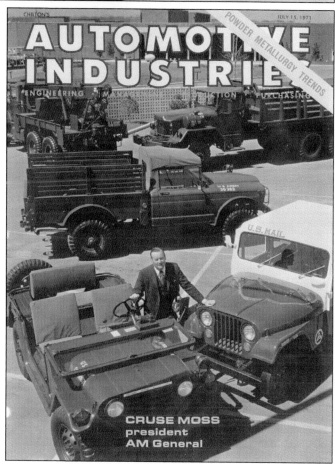

An M151A2 is seen here on a special Engineering Department testing machine dubbed "the shaker." Its four hydraulic rams operate individually to replicate the worst off-road driving experiences and to shake the vehicle until something breaks or falls off, thus identifying potential problem areas so they can be beefed up. AM General used a similar device to test its commercial buses.

The M151 and M151A2 Mutts are often confused with the World War II Jeep, but they share no parts and are only related by their common manufacturers. Put them side by side, and they scarcely resemble each other. The Willys Jeep was the World War II and Korean War vehicle, and the M151 and M151A2 were Vietnam-era vehicles.

With its high ground clearance and agile four-wheel independent suspension, the M151A2 was a highly capable off-road vehicle in any kind of terrain. The M151A2 and the larger M715 one-and-a-quarter-ton truck were eventually replaced by the Humvee.

The veteran M151A2 Mutt is most at home in desolate places far from paved roads. It excels in difficult terrain. Rugged and dependable, the M151A2 Mutts served the Army well.

This heavy-duty M36A2 is a two-and-a-half-ton truck produced during 1970, when the business unit was still called the General Products Division of American Motors. The division became AM General Corporation in March 1971. This particular truck model is a cargo/personnel carrier, one of more than 35 distinct body and chassis configurations available in the M36A2 series.

AM General's two-and-a-half-ton truck was dubbed the "workhorse of the Army" and was one of the highest-volume products the company built. These trucks were assembled at the South Bend plant, with the cargo bodies fabricated at the nearby Mishawaka plant.

Over the years, AM General's South Bend plant produced a wide range of military trucks, including light-duty quarter-ton Mutts and DJ-5s, along with medium-duty two-and-a-half-ton, heavy-duty five-ton, and giant 14-ton units. AM General still produces more light tactical vehicles than any other company in the world.

The military vehicles manufactured by AM General are sold to the US government and also to friendly forces around the world, making the company a major exporter of American products. The company has an extensive support network to supply spare parts and service instruction around the globe.

The ubiquitous AM General DJ-5 Dispatcher, a two-wheel-drive light truck that got its start as a postal vehicle, was also offered in this military version. In this capacity, it was utilized as a low-cost staff car, communication vehicle, and patrol car for military police.

While mechanically similar to the postal trucks, the military DJ-5 Dispatcher did have some alterations to make it more suitable for its role. The vehicle was offered in both left- and right-hand steering versions.

Many people wonder what the mysterious T.P. 18 and T.P. 24 writing above the DJ-5's wheels means. It is simple—tire pressure. Having it painted above the tire helps ensure the correct pressures will be maintained.

The rear door of the Army DJ-5 Dispatcher vehicle swings out sideways for loading cargo into the back. A rear seat can also be specified to make it a command car.

Here is the M45A2, a two-and-a-half-ton six-by-six chassis truck, around 1980. This powerful brute rode a 154-inch wheelbase and was powered by an inline six-cylinder multi-fuel engine. The fuel tank's capacity was 50 gallons.

The tough M45A2 weighed 11,350 pounds and could haul up to 13,000. Top speed was 54 miles per hour, and the vehicle had a cruising range of 275 miles. These trucks are mostly out of service now but available in the used truck market. They are very popular with military vehicle collectors.

Shown here is another South Bend defense product, the AM General M814 long cargo truck, a five-ton six-by-six heavy hauler. This unit weighed nearly 25,000 pounds and was designed for carrying large, heavy loads on-road or off.

One look at the rear of this vehicle shows why it is called a long cargo truck. It rode a 215-inch wheelbase and was a whisker over 377 inches long. Powered by a 240-horsepower six-cylinder diesel engine, it had a top speed of 52 miles per hour and could climb a 38 percent grade.

The biggest trucks produced thus far by AM General were the M915 series six-by-four 14-ton units. These massive trucks utilized a Crane Carrier Corporation cab—the CCC badge can be seen in the grille. The gross vehicle weight rating was 50,000 pounds, with a gross combination truck and trailer rating of 105,000 pounds. Power was via a big 14-liter inline six-cylinder turbo diesel engine.

Heavy tactical vehicles that break down or are damaged in action require a powerful, heavy-duty wrecker to bring them home, and AM General built this handsome five-ton wrecker for that job.

Here is another version of the popular DJ-5 Dispatcher quarter-ton truck, this one produced for the US Navy. These were used for onshore communications as well as for MP duty. They were compact, fuel efficient, and inexpensive to purchase.

Note that this particular unit does not carry an outside spare tire, allowing easier access to the rear cargo door. The roof vent is to help provide ventilation. These trucks were powered by an American Motors six-cylinder engine driving through an automatic transmission.

In the mid-1990s, AM General offered a vehicle update and renewal service called the Extended Service Program (ESP), in which existing two-and-a-half-ton military trucks were brought back to South Bend for a complete rebuild and refurbishment, thus extending their service life by a considerable amount at a great savings in cost versus purchasing new trucks.

This Army two-and-a-half-ton cargo/personnel carrier has its top and windshield folded to be transported by air. The huge Lockheed C-5 Galaxy aircraft seen in the photograph can carry several trucks with ease.

Another AM General military truck is shown here fitted with a Koenig utility body complete with ladder racks and diamond-plate rear-step bumper. The truck is probably a Toledo-built M715 or an AM725, either one a light-duty vehicle based on the Jeep J-series trucks.

On March 22, 1983, the US Army Tank-Automotive Command awarded a contract to AM General for the production of a new vehicle the company had designed and developed: the M998 Series High-Mobility Multi-Purpose Wheeled Vehicle (HMMWV), which was known initially as the Hummer, then came to be called the Humvee.

The HMMWV contract was the largest contract for tactical wheeled vehicles ever awarded by the US Army to that time, calling for about 55,000 vehicles in the initial contract. And do not bother trying to tip over a Humvee. The vehicle is designed to perform well on a 30 percent side slope at its gross combined weight, which is the weight of the vehicle, passengers, fuel, and cargo. Head on, it can tackle a 40 percent grade.

The Humvee is truly a multipurpose vehicle; among its many roles, it serves as a troop carrier, scout car, missile launcher (shown here), cargo truck, command vehicle, and more.

The Humvee's designers put a great deal of thought into the vehicle. For instance, the windshield is slanted forward to reduce reflective glare that might alert an enemy. This vehicle has its lights covered as well. The flat hood makes a handy map table.

This 1986 AM General Humvee is configured as a cargo truck, a popular and useful body type. These rugged vehicles are designed to present the lowest possible profile via gear drive hubs that reduce the chassis and body height.

Stripped down for special operations, the Humvee can carry several heavy machine guns into action, making it an extremely lethal assault vehicle. It can also conquer nearly any sort of terrain in its scouting and attack mission.

This Humvee, a slant-back body type configured for desert use, has added unarmored doors. The wheels and tires are equipped with special sensors and piping so that the air pressure can be modulated for on- or off-road driving.

A cargo-truck-type Humvee with a hard box and armored doors with ballistic glass, this one is painted for non-desert areas. Humvees are available with different levels of ballistic and explosion protection depending on the mission. Non-armored Humvees can be "up-armored" in the field if necessary.

Not many tactical vehicles can boast the fording ability of the AM General Humvee. The vehicle can reliably ford 30 inches of water in standard form and 60 inches of water with the Deep Fording Kit. Ground clearance is a full 17 inches.

Wearing camouflage paint for jungle use, this slant-back Humvee represents a fairly standard variation of the vehicle. AM General has been building these machines in South Bend since the early 1980s.

A pair of tough Humvees on desert patrol, keeping America protected.

In late 1988, Vice Pres. George Herbert Walker Bush visited the AM General facilities in South Bend and Mishawaka. In this photograph, the vice president speaks to assembled Humvee workers inside the plant, thanking them for their hard work and dedication in providing the Army with the tools it needs.

Another view of the vice president speaking to AM General employees shows how close they were to him as he spoke, a level of intimacy not usually seen in these appearances. The Humvee, of course, rose to international fame during the Gulf War's two major operations: Desert Shield and Desert Storm.

Vice Pres. George H.W. Bush speaks with AM General president George Maddox outside the Humvee plant during his 1988 visit to the area. The Humvee is parked there for a reason—Maddox wants Bush to take it for a test drive.

With Vice President Bush at the wheel of the Humvee, a smiling George Maddox climbs aboard. Note the AM General tactical trucks in the background. The company was anxious to show off all its production vehicles to the vice president.

Vice President Bush snaps off a few instructions just before driving off. The man seated in the rear is not identified but may be a secret service agent. The Humvee is always ready for any job, with a rated payload of 4,000 pounds for the base model 1151 and a towed load allowance of 4,000 pounds.

Vice President Bush drives a Humvee. Riding a 130-inch wheelbase and boasting a 91-inch width, the Humvee takes up a lot of real estate. Although it is 194 inches long, its turning radius is only 25 feet, not much more than a compact car.

Vice President Bush, inside AM General headquarters, admires a mounted display model given to him as a souvenir of his visit to the plant. A war veteran himself, Bush had great empathy with the men and women of America's armed forces.

Here is a rarely seen version of the Humvee: a military cabover cargo truck. The cabover Humvee was offered for a time in both military and civilian versions, but the idea never caught on.

THE IDEAL ADMINISTRATIVE SUPPORT VEHICLE

◤◢ AM General
World Class Capability

This AM General brochure for the military version of the DJ-5 is a hard one to find. The DJ-5 was one of the few two-wheel-drive vehicles AM General produced. This particular sales brochure was produced by American Motors when it owned the company. The year of this DJ-5 model is 1982.

Here are two views of the AM General M718A1 quarter-ton four-by-four ambulance. A variation of the M151A1 Mutt military scout car, this vehicle was designed to evacuate wounded soldiers from the front lines, taking them to initial aid stations. Many lives have been saved because of the speed and cross-country agility of these rugged trucks.

The South Bend–produced AM General Humvee has become an enduring symbol of American strength and resolve and a guardian of freedom. Engineered for reliability, it is practically impervious to the signal-jamming and electronics-interference attacks that will be a big part of tomorrow's battlefields.

Set up for jungle camouflage and mounting a swivel for a machine gun on the roof, this Humvee is ready for anything.

Here is an interesting Humvee configuration; it is set up to carry four troops seated in the back on sideways-facing benches plus two in the regular rear seats, two up front, and one man standing with his weapon at the ready.

Note the amazing ground clearance as well as the extra-heavy-duty A-arms of the front suspension. Like the proverbial anvil, the Humvee is built for rugged use and long life.

AM General also produces all the engines used in the Humvee through one of its subsidiaries, General Engine Products. The engines are powerful V8 diesels capable of propelling the Humvee along at 70 miles per hour with a 250-mile cruising range.

Another AM General subsidiary, General Transmission Products, produces the heavy-duty four-speed automatic transmissions used in the Humvee. Over the years, AM General has continuously improved the Humvee, giving it much more horsepower and a stronger frame and suspension. Its towing and carrying capacity have also been increased along the way.

One of the newest configurations for the Humvee is as a mobile artillery platform. This photograph shows the ultra mobile Humvee Hawkeye 105-millimeter self-propelled howitzer weapon system. AM General is working on further vehicle-mounted weapons systems structured around soft recoil technology.

The advantages of the Humvee-mounted artillery are easy to understand. Rather than utilizing a truck to tow an artillery gun, which must be parked and set up prior to firing, the Humvee drives right into position, and the crew can get into action much faster, increasing the weapon's lethality.

The M1167 is an expanded-capacity TOW or armament carrier Humvee. It provides superior protection for crew, weapons, components, and ammunition. Along with the TOW missile launcher, the M1167 also provides for the ring-mounting and firing of various weapons systems with a 360-degree arc of fire. The M1167 is able to stow up to six TOW missiles in the cargo area and is available with a manual traversing unit and a TOW gunners protection kit.

Pictured here is a Humvee equipped with the Enhanced Tactical Lethality (ETL) kit. The kit adds greater flexibility for the Army's current HMMWV inventory. This added lethality is available for cavalry, scout, and weapons company missions and includes the M230LF 30-millimeter weapon seen here. This versatile gun is capable of firing M778, M789, and NATO rounds.

The Humvee M1165 is designed for special operations and is shown here in desert trim and bristling with machine guns. Built to provide optimal protection for crew, weapons components, and ammunition, the M1165 is expertly engineered to withstand the demanding requirements of special operation missions that necessitate increased payloads without sacrificing mobility, dependability, or performance.

This Humvee has a protective enclosure for its top-mounted gun. There are more than 300,000 AM General–produced Humvee vehicles in service around the globe, making it the most ubiquitous military vehicle on earth.

In response to requests from the military, AM General has engineered this special narrow-body Humvee designed for transport inside a military helicopter rather than underneath on a sling.

It is a tight fit, but having the ability to be carried inside the helicopter makes it much easier to transport versus the old-fashioned sling carrier. The soldiers need to duck down as the vehicle enters but can remain in the Humvee, ready to deploy as soon as they land.

A Humvee special ops vehicle charging across the desert sands with five heavy machine guns blazing is a highly effective assault weapon. Is it any wonder the Humvee remains a popular choice with armies around the world?

The enormous power of the Humvee's V8 diesel engine—380 pound-feet of torque at a low 1,700 rpm and 190 horsepower at 3,400 rpm—along with its ability to cross nearly any kind of terrain makes it a very potent special ops vehicle.

One of the latest products to appear from AM General is this new light tactical vehicle concept by AM General and Jeep. The Jeep Gladiator Extreme Military-Grade Truck (XMT) is the first phase of a collaboration that reunites two companies whose histories trace back to World War II. In creating the Jeep Gladiator XMT, AM General leveraged the Gladiator's class-leading capabilities and customized the truck to meet global customers' needs for a light-weight military truck.

In all, AM General has produced more than 1.5 million vehicles, and they have been deployed in more than 70 countries worldwide. The company and its predecessors boast a long—more than 150 years—and proud history serving the nation. This Multi-Purpose Truck (MPT) was designed to allow customers to configure payload modules customized to their specific needs. Variants can include the two-man with flatbed, two-plus-six personnel carrier, four-man base with cargo box, and nine-crew capacity vehicle. The MPT provides a multipurpose platform capable of integrating a multitude of modules, weapons, and additional internal components.

Six

THEY ALSO SERVED

"Ball Band" Rubber and Woolen Mfg. Co., Mishawaka, Indiana

The Mishawaka Woolen Manufacturing Company was incorporated in 1874 to produce red flannel boots with a black band around the top. After a red ball was added to the band, the Ball Band trademark was created, and locals began calling the firm the "Ball Band Company." In 1923, it was renamed the Mishawaka Rubber and Woolen Manufacturing Company. During World War II, the company manufactured the vital rubber cells for self-sealing fuel tanks used on military aircraft. It also produced special extra-large bladder cells for the bombers used in the famed "30 Seconds over Tokyo" raid by Gen. Jimmy Doolittle and his airmen. Ball Band also made thousands of raincoats, water repellent pants, and boots for the Army.

The Malleable Steel Range Manufacturing Company incorporated in 1898. The firm produced coal and wood cooking ranges, in time expanding into commercial cooking ranges as well. The business was eventually renamed the South Bend Range Corporation.

Like many civilian producers, during World War II the company converted to war production, manufacturing oil ranges and bake ovens for the Army and Navy. In fact, the US Navy equipped nearly all of its ships with South Bend cooking stoves. The company is still in business as a division of the Middleby Corporation in North Carolina.

Established by Wallace Dodge on the banks of the St. Joseph River in June 1878, the Dodge Manufacturing Company produced wooden sawbucks, chopping bowls, and a popular wagon jack. Before long, the company was also producing its patented wood split pully and rope drives to drive machinery in factories. Starting in a small wood-frame building, the company eventually expanded into the large plant seen here.

During World War II, the Dodge Manufacturing Company produced thousands of marine bearings and stern tubes for ships, including for the famous C3 ships and the Victory ships. The plant also produced thousands of shipping containers for the B-17 aircraft engines being produced by the Studebaker Corporation. Of 388 Dodge employees serving in the armed forces during the war, 12 were killed in action.

Begun in the mid-1800s by Scottish immigrant James Oliver, the company that became known as the Oliver Chilled Plow Works was most famous for the greatly improved cast-iron plow it produced. By 1900, the company was the largest plow manufacturer in the world. In 1929, it merged with four other agricultural implement producers to become the Oliver Farm Equipment Corporation. Throughout its history, it produced a variety of items for the US military.

Like so many other American companies, when World War II started, Oliver converted to military production. From 1941 to 1943, Oliver produced guns and shells for the war effort. From 1943 to the end of the war, the South Bend plant served as a government depot and warehouse.

A small home-based business started in 1896 by F.G. "Bucktail" Worden, inventor of the Bucktail lure, was incorporated in 1909 as the South Bend Bait Company. The firm grew rapidly and by 1910 had 50 women working on the assembly line and 15 full-time salesmen. During World War II, the company was a subcontractor to several major producers, manufacturing small machined parts for gauges, speedometers, and instruments. It also produced screw machine parts for turrets built by Bendix Aviation.

Established in 1874, the South Bend Toy Company began in a small rented room near the East Race in downtown South Bend before moving into a larger facility in 1876. Among other things, it manufactured doll carriages and croquet sets. During World War II, the firm turned to making wooden tent stakes and tent poles, producing four million of them during the war years. It also made full-size baby carriages needed by the thousands of women working in defense factories and more than 150,00 nightsticks used by military police.

Organized in 1905 as the Bantam Ball Bearing Company in Bantam, Connecticut, the operation moved to a new plant in South Bend in July 1928. In 1935, it became a wholly owned subsidiary of the Torrington Bearing Company of Torrington, Connecticut. Success came rapidly. By 1940, the South Bend workforce had grown from 55 employees to 375. During World War II, the firm produced a wide variety of bearings for everything from aircraft instruments to heavy naval gun mounts that used 121-inch bearings.

MEETING THE NEED
FOR NON-MAGNETIC AND NON-CORROSIVE BEARINGS

Working with many materials — Monel, Beryllium Copper, 440-C Stainless Steel and Cobalt Alloys — Torrington is continually developing higher capacities and longer life in anti-friction bearings for unusually demanding applications. Many of these applications call for non-magnetic or non-corrosive properties — and often both in the same bearing.

For example, in submarine rudder posts and instruments, good bearing performance often depends as much on corrosion and magnetic resistance as on the load-carrying capacity. In sensitive electronic equipment, valves and other mechanical applications, special metals may be necessary to eliminate undesirable magnetic effects.

Designing and manufacturing bearings to meet unusual requirements is a Torrington specialty. Developments in non-magnetic and corrosion-resistant bearings are a part of Torrington's continuing effort to improve bearings in design, metallurgy and performance.

THE TORRINGTON COMPANY
South Bend 21, Indiana • Torrington, Connecticut
PROGRESS THROUGH PRECISION—IN BEARING DESIGN AND PERFORMANCE

By March 1941, the Torrington Bearing Company plant in South Bend was put on a wartime schedule, working seven days a week, 24 hours a day to meet the demand for critically needed bearings. By that point, 100 percent of its production was for the war effort. It became the first of 174 Indiana defense plants to win the coveted Army-Navy E for Excellence Award.

Miles Laboratories, famed maker of Alka Seltzer, was called on by the US Army during World War II to utilize its expertise in packaging those handy tablets in foil packs. Miles was contracted to produce millions of K ration kits containing coffee, lemonade, orange juice, bouillon, and other soluble items. Some of the supply ships carrying these to the European theater were sunk by German submarines. Years later, foil-wrapped coffee packs washed up on beaches in Britain and were still perfectly fresh.

The Fuller-O'Brien Paint Company (formerly the O'Brien Corporation) had a long history in South Bend producing paints, varnishes, and other such products. As might be guessed, during World War II, the company produced a variety of flat paints and varnishes for camouflage as well as paint for bombs and service equipment. The company was bought out by Uniroyal and today is located at 2001 West Washington Street in South Bend.

The Wilson Brothers Shirt Company was established as a haberdashery and custom shirt maker in 1863 in Chicago. In 1866, it moved manufacturing to South Bend. When World War II erupted, the company was put to work manufacturing shirts for the Army. Although it had more than 1,600 workers at the time and could produce up to 30,000 pieces of clothing per day, it needed to hire more to boost production.

The Wilson Brothers Shirt Company went into decline soon after the war ended and, despite a merger with Enro Shirt Company, had to close its doors in the mid-1970s.

Stromberg Carburetor was a longtime division of Bendix Corporation. The company manufactured critical aircraft carburetors, designing several new high-altitude models for the advanced fighters and bombers that were introduced during the war.

The Singer Sewing Machine Company established a plant in South Bend in 1868 to produce sewing machine cabinets, which were shipped to plants in New Jersey, Britain, and Europe for final assembly of the machine works. The company had a mixed history in World War II. It produced cabinets for Army sewing machines and packing cases for the .45-caliber pistols its New Jersey plant produced but failed to sell the Army Air Force on its idea for wooden propellers or any other big contract proposals.

The Stephenson Underwear Mills' historic three-story textile mill in South Bend was constructed in anticipation of producing underwear for the armed forces of World War I and was part of a larger nine-building complex. The building was used for carding, spinning, sewing, cutting, and knitting. As one of the largest manufacturers of underwear in the country, Stephenson Underwear Mills was an important supplier to the US military during World War I. The mill continued to prosper up until the stock market crash of 1929. After that, the building was used by several companies, and today, it is the Stephenson Mills Apartments.

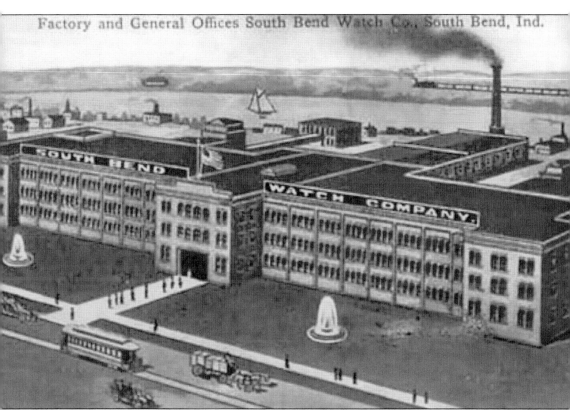

Factory and General Offices South Bend Watch Co., South Bend, Ind.

During World War I, the South Bend Watch Company supplied small gun parts and components to several gun manufacturers. The company went out of business in 1933, so it did not participate in the effort during World War II.

DISCOVER THOUSANDS OF LOCAL HISTORY BOOKS FEATURING MILLIONS OF VINTAGE IMAGES

Arcadia Publishing, the leading local history publisher in the United States, is committed to making history accessible and meaningful through publishing books that celebrate and preserve the heritage of America's people and places.

Find more books like this at
www.arcadiapublishing.com

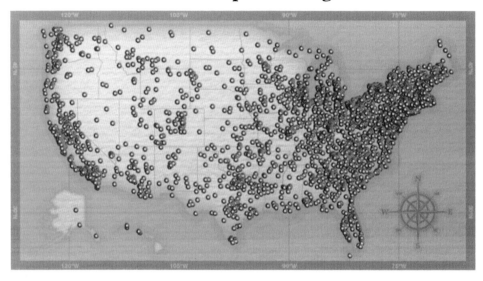

Search for your hometown history, your old stomping grounds, and even your favorite sports team.

Consistent with our mission to preserve history on a local level, this book was printed in South Carolina on American-made paper and manufactured entirely in the United States. Products carrying the accredited Forest Stewardship Council (FSC) label are printed on 100 percent FSC-certified paper.

MADE IN THE